Children's Man Method

MW00581175

by William Bay

Recommended Mel Bay Supplements:
Beginning Mandolin Solos [MB94884BCD]
Easiest Mandolin Book [MB94833]
Children's Mandolin Chord Book [MB21500]

Audio Contents

1 Tuning the Mandolin	31 Bile Dem Cabbage Down
2 The C Chord	32 I am Bound for the Promised Land
3 C Strumming	33 The Hope
4 Three Blind Mice	34 3rd String, Whole Notes
5 Row, Row, Row Your Boat	35 3rd String, Half Notes
6 C-G7 Strum	36 3rd String, Quarter Notes
7 London Bridge	37 Old Chisholm Trail
8 This Old Man	38 Morning Song
9 Cowboy's Song	39 Cripple Creek
10 Pop Goes the Weasel	40 Early Christmas Morn
11 He's Got the Whole World	41 4th String, Whole Notes
12 Buffalo Gals	42 4th String, Half Notes
13 Polly Wolly Doodle	43 4th String, Quarter Notes
14 Brother John	44 Wildwood Flower
15 The Farmer in the Dell	45 I Ride an Old Paint
16 Oh, Bury Me Not on the Lone Prarie	46 Early American Hymn
17 Banks of the Ohio	47 Will the Circle be Unbroken
18 Amazing Grace	48 Mama Don't Allow
19 The F Chord	49 Streets of Laredo
20 Camptown Races	50 In the Pines
21 Li'l Liza Jane	51 Come and Go with Me
22 1st String, Whole Notes	52 Golden Slippers
23 1st String, Half Notes	53 Minor Song
24 1st String, Quarter Notes	54 Green Grow The Lilacs
25 1st String, Eighth Notes	55 This Train
26 1st String Songs	56 It Ain't Gonna Rain No More
27 2nd String, Whole Notes	57 Jacob's Ladder
28 2nd String, Half Notes	58 All The Pretty Little Horses
29 2nd String, Quarter Notes	59 Angel Band
30 2nd String, Running the Notes	

1 2 3 4 5 6 7 8 9 0

© 2012 BY MEL BAY PUBLICATIONS, INC., PACIFIC, MO 63069.
ALL RIGHTS RESERVED. INTERNATIONAL COPYRIGHT SECURED. B.M.I. MADE AND PRINTED IN U.S.A.
No part of this publication may be reproduced in whole or in part, or stored in a retrieval system, or transmitted in any form
or by any means, electronic, mechanical, photocopy, recording, or otherwise, without written permission of the publisher.

Visit us on the Web at www.melbay.com — E-mail us at email@melbay.com

Table of Contents

Tuning the Mandolin

1. Listen to Track 1 on the audio. Tune each string to the recorded string of the same pitch. 🔊
Track 1

2. Electronic Tuners
I highly recommend that you obtain an electronic tuner for your mandolin. This device will show you if each string is out of tune and will also let you know how to adjust it to get it back in tune.

Holding the Mandolin

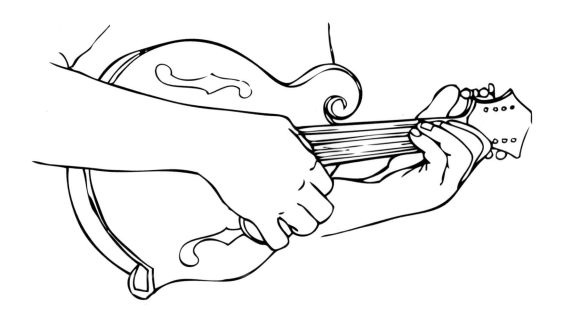

Holding the Pick

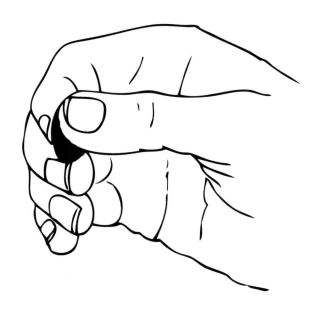

How to Read Chord Diagrams

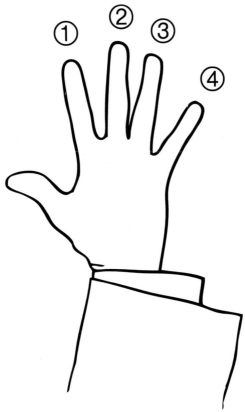

Left-Hand Fingers

Play strings open

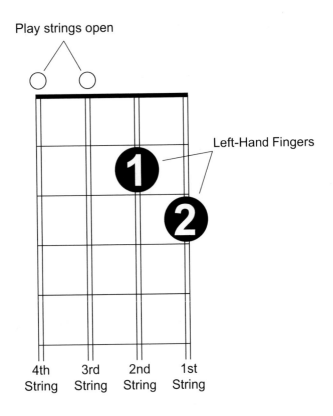

Left-Hand Fingers

4th String   3rd String   2nd String   1st String

Time Signatures

$\frac{4}{4}$ or **C** = Common Time

Four strums or beats per measure.

C

$\frac{3}{4}$ = Three-four or Waltz Time

Three strums or beats per measure.

C

C Chord

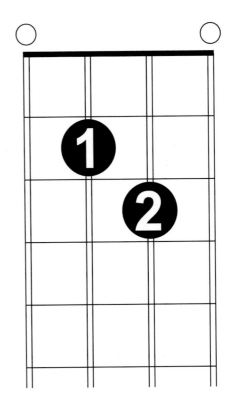

/ = Down Strum – from large strings to small

C Strumming

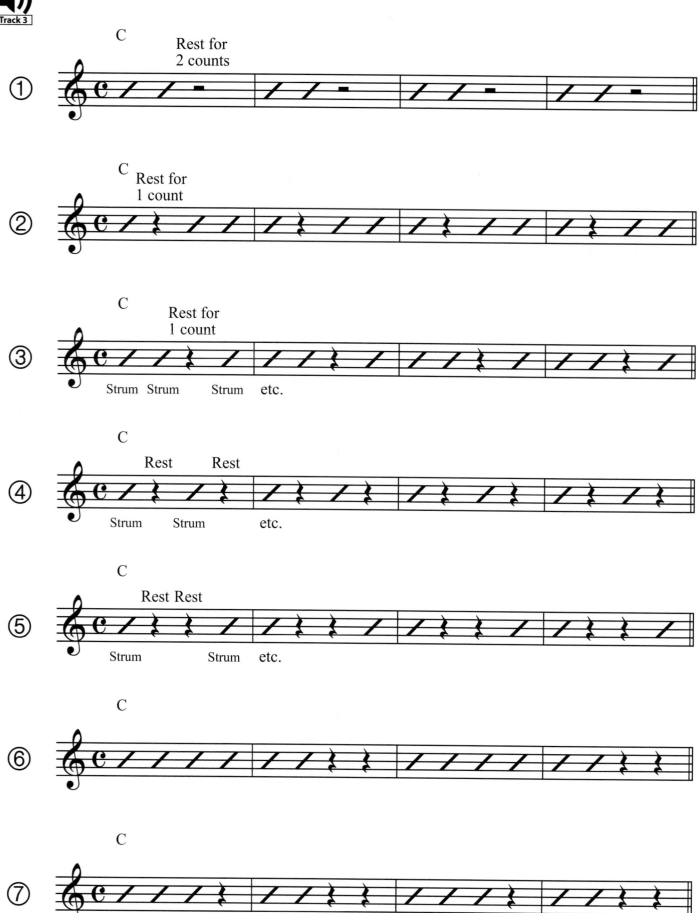

8

Three Blind Mice

Sing and Play

Row, Row, Row Your Boat

Sing and Play

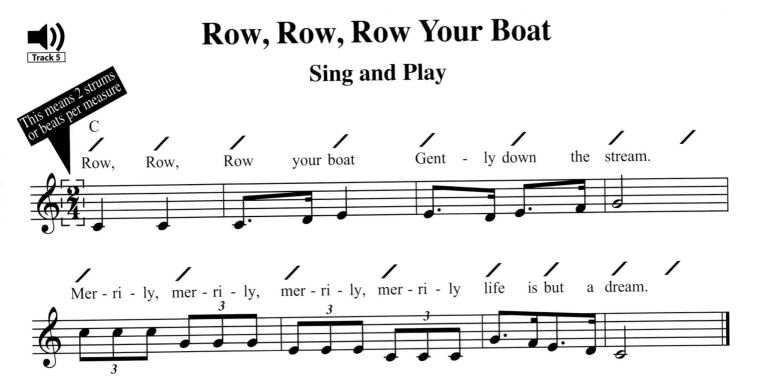

G7 Chord

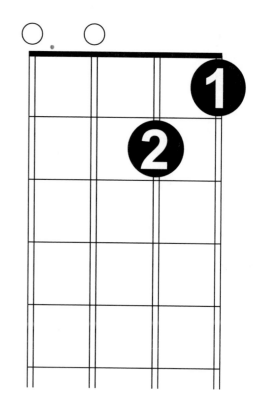

C–G7 Strum

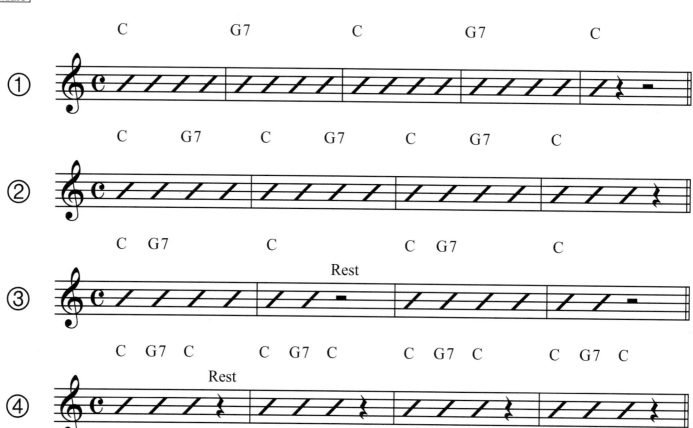

10

London Bridge

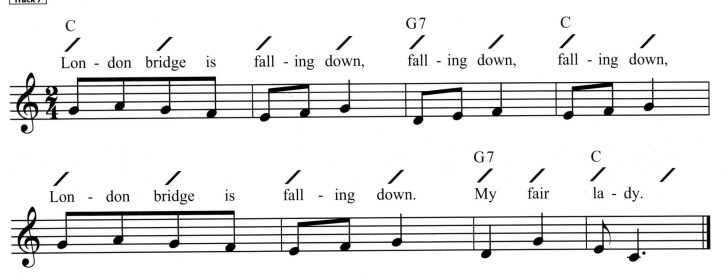

This Old Man

11

3/4 Time

Up 'til now, we have played either 4 strums per measure ($\frac{4}{4}$ or $\mathbf{c}$) or 2 strums per measure ($\frac{2}{4}$). Now we will play 3 strums per measure ($\frac{3}{4}$).

Cowboy's Song

Track 9

Count 1-2-3, 1-2-3, etc.

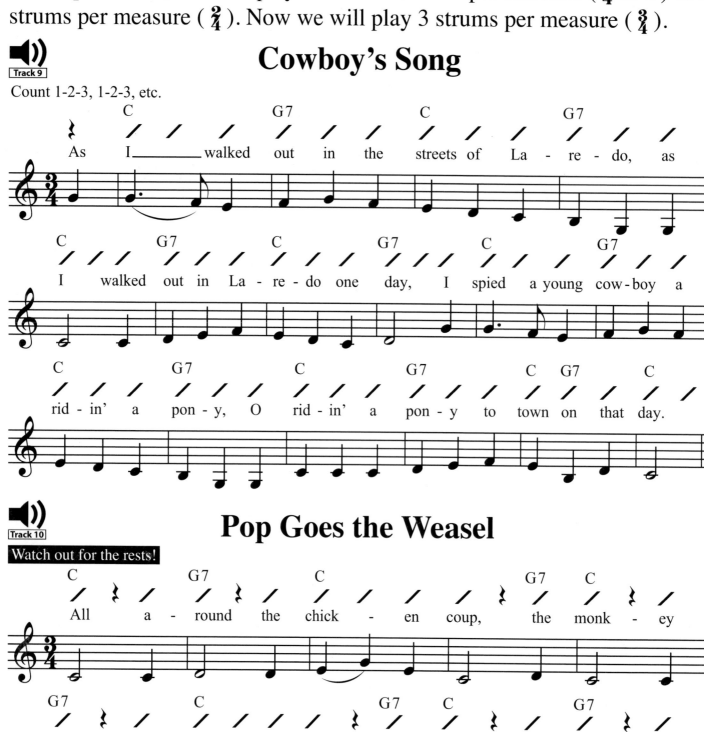

Pop Goes the Weasel

Track 10

Watch out for the rests!

12

He's Got the Whole World

Buffalo Gals

13

Polly Wolly Doodle

G Chord

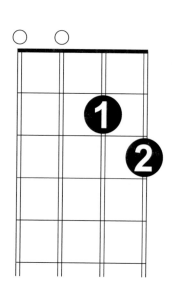

Brother John

Sing and Play

G
Are you sleep-ing? Are you sleep-ing? Bro-ther John. Bro-ther John.

Morn-ing bells are ring-ing! Morn-ing bells are ring-ing! Din-dan-don. Din-dan-don.

D7 Chord

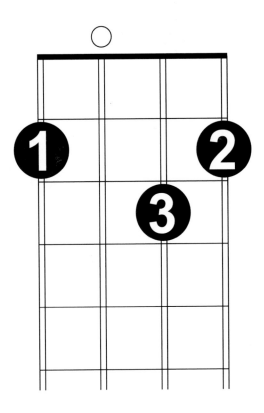

The Farmer in the Dell

Track 15

Folk Song

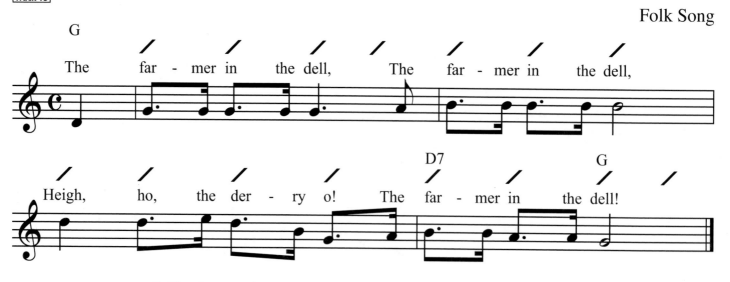

2. The farmer takes a wife
3. The wife takes a child
4. The child takes a nurse
5. The nurse takes a dog

6. The dog takes a cat.
7. The cat takes a rat.
8. The rat takes the cheese.
9. The cheese stands alone.

Oh, Bury Me Not on the Lone Prairie

Track 16

Banks of the Ohio

17

F Chord

 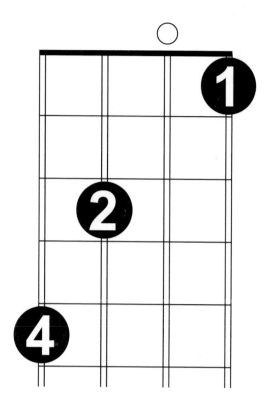

If the F chord is difficult, start by playing only the top two strings. Then add the third and eventually the fourth string.

Track 19

Strum

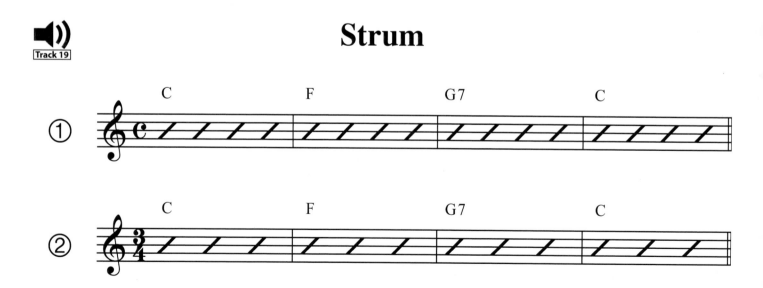

Camptown Races

Li'l Liza Jane

19

Learning Notes

1st String (E)

E

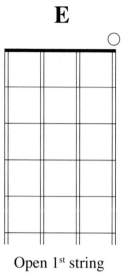

Open 1st string

E

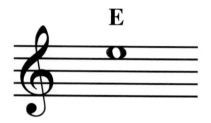

Open 1st string

F

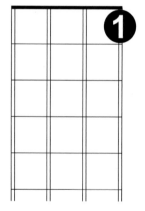

1st Finger, 1st Fret, 1st string

F

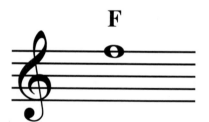

1st Finger, 1st Fret, 1st string

G

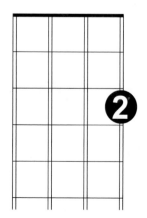

2nd Finger, 3rd Fret, 1st string

G

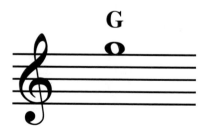

2nd Finger, 3rd Fret, 1st string

Types of Notes

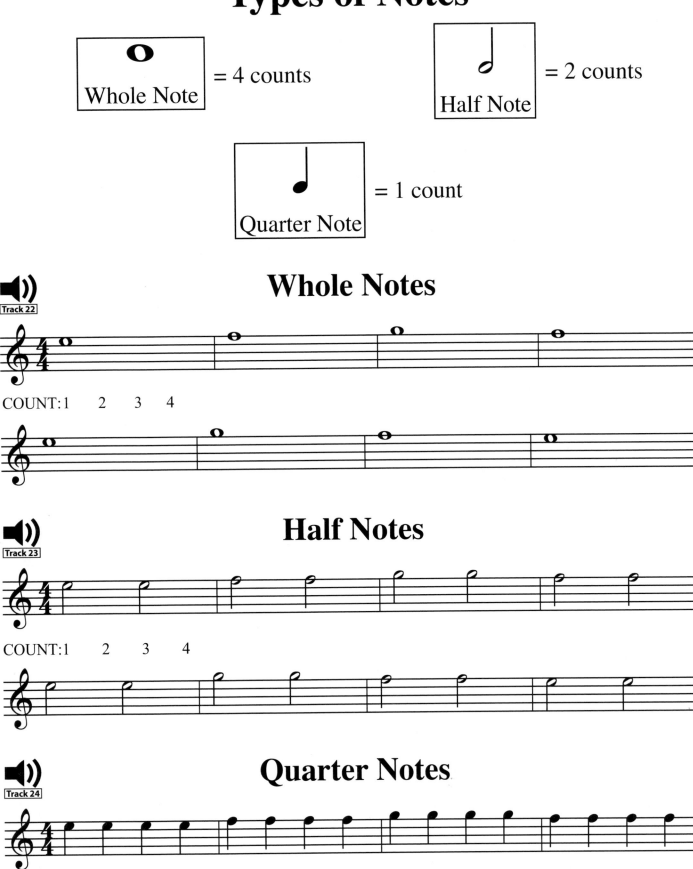

Whole Note = 4 counts

Half Note = 2 counts

Quarter Note = 1 count

Whole Notes

Track 22

COUNT: 1   2   3   4

Half Notes

Track 23

COUNT: 1   2   3   4

Quarter Notes

Track 24

COUNT: 1   2   3   4

Rest

Eighth Notes

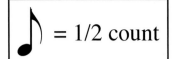 

Track 25

I Love Eating Donuts
Say and Play

I love eat-ing do-nuts!   I love eat-ing do-nuts!   I love eat-ing do-nuts!   I love eat-ing do-nuts!

Don't Step on Alligators
Say and Play

Don't step on al-li-ga-tors! Don't step on al-li-ga-tors! Don't step on al-li-ga-tors! Don't step on al-li-ga-tors!

F is Fred, Now Scratch Your Head

F   is   Fred   now   scratch   your   head.   F   is   fred   now   scratch   your   head.

Eating Cookies Makes Me Happy
Say and Play

Eat - ing   cook - ies   makes   me   hap - py,   Eat - ing   cook - ies   makes   me   hap - py,

Eat - ing   cook - ies   makes   me   hap - py,   Eat - ing   cook - ies   makes   me   hap - py.

G is Gail, Go Pet a Whale!

G   is   Gail,   go   pet   a   whale!   G   is   Gail,   go   pet   a   whale!

Track 26

Won't You Climb the Stairs with Me

Chasing Rabbits

Up We Go in My Balloon

See Saw

Gliding

Picking Study

Review Song

Notes on the 2nd (A) String

A

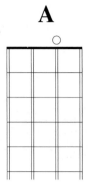

2nd String Open

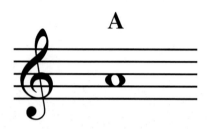

A

2nd String Open

B

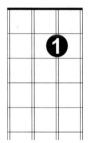

1st Finger, 2nd String, 2nd Fret

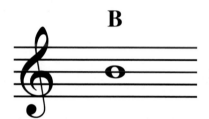

B

1st Finger, 2nd String, 2nd Fret

C

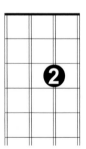

2nd Finger, 2nd String, 3rd Fret

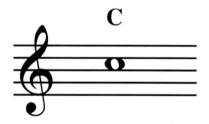

C

2nd Finger, 2nd String, 3rd Fret

D

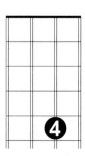

3rd or 4th Finger (little finger), 2nd String, 5th Fret

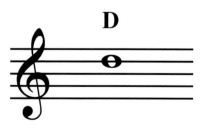

D

4th Finger, 2nd String, 5th Fret
(3rd finger may be used)

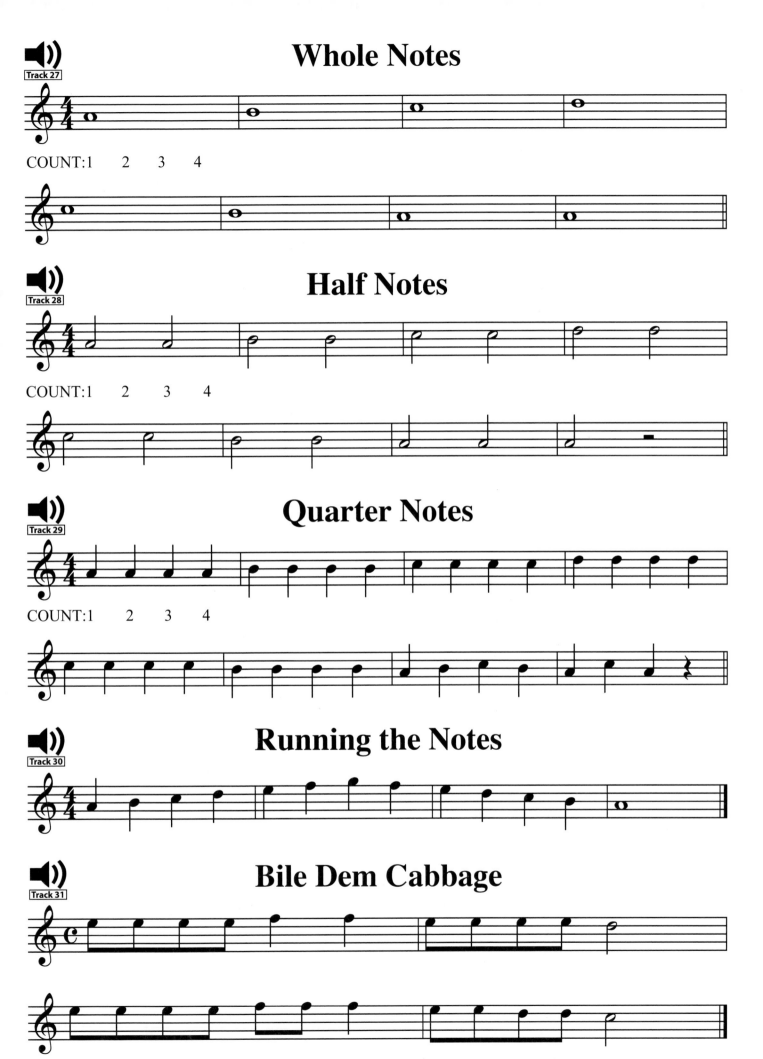

High A

High A

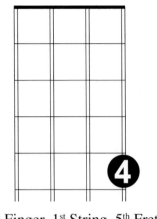

4th Finger, 1st String, 5th Fret

High A

4th Finger, 1st String, 5th Fret

I am Bound for the Promised Land

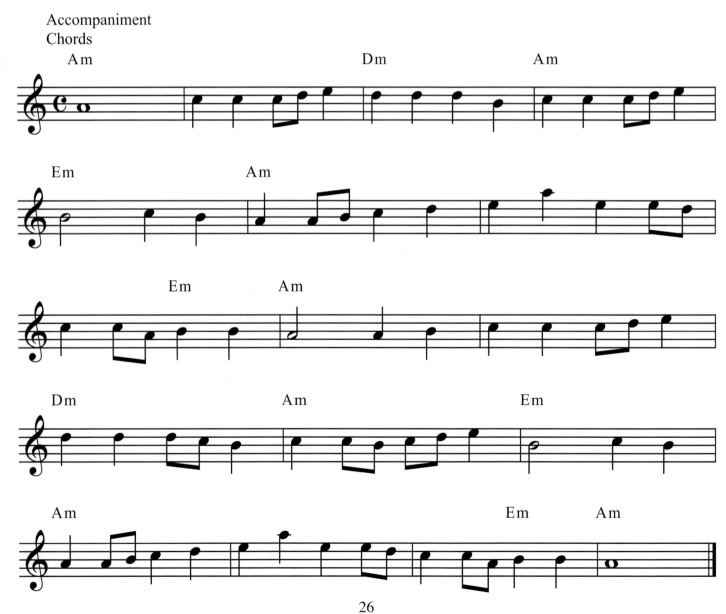

Repeat Sign

A Repeat Sign means to go back and play again the music found between the repeat signs.

The Hope

Notes on the 3rd (D) String

D

3rd String Open

D

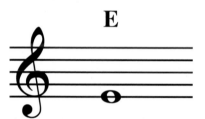

3rd String Open

E

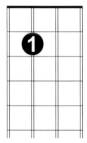

1st Finger, 3rd String, 2nd Fret

E

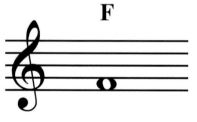

1st Finger, 3rd String, 2nd Fret

F

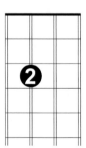

2nd Finger, 3rd String, 3rd Fret

F

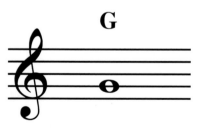

2nd Finger, 3rd String, 3rd Fret

G

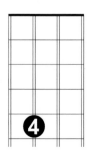

3rd or 4th Finger, 3rd String, 5th Fret

G

3rd or 4th Finger, 3rd String, 5th Fret

Whole Notes

COUNT:1   2   3   4

Half Notes

Track 35

COUNT:1   2   3   4

Rest

Quarter Notes

Track 36

COUNT:1   2   3   4

Rest

Old Chisholm Trail

Track 37

Accompaniment
Chords

*   Notes which start a tune before the first full measure are called "Pickup Notes." Their time value is subtracted from the last measure of the song.

29

Dotted Half Note

A dotted half note receives 3 counts.

Morning Song

Track 38

Moderately

Accompaniment Chords

Cripple Creek

Track 39

Fast

Accompaniment Chords

Early Christmas Morn

Track 40

Gently

Accompaniment Chords

30

Notes on the 4ᵗʰ (G) String

Low G

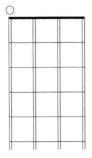

4ᵗʰ String Open

Low G

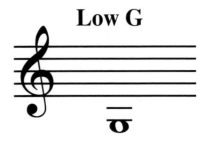

4ᵗʰ String Open

Low A

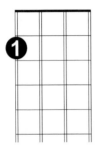

1ˢᵗ Finger, 4ᵗʰ String, 2ⁿᵈ Fret

Low A

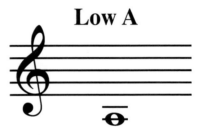

1ˢᵗ Finger, 4ᵗʰ String, 2ⁿᵈ Fret

Low B

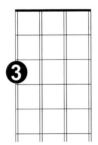

2ⁿᵈ or 3ʳᵈ Finger, 4ᵗʰ String, 3ʳᵈ Fret

Low B

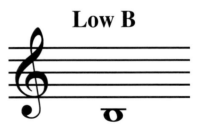

2ⁿᵈ or 3ʳᵈ Finger, 4ᵗʰ String, 3ʳᵈ Fret

Low C

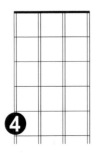

3ʳᵈ or 4ᵗʰ Finger, 4ᵗʰ String, 5ᵗʰ Fret

Low C

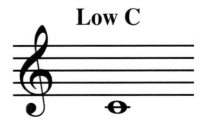

3ʳᵈ or 4ᵗʰ Finger, 4ᵗʰ String, 5ᵗʰ Fret

31

Whole Notes

Track 41

Half Notes

Track 42

Quarter Notes

Track 43

Wildwood Flower

Track 44

Accompaniment
Chords

Dotted Quarter Note

A dotted quarter note receives 1 1/2 counts.

I Ride an Old Paint

Early American Hymn

The Tie

When two notes are tied together you pick the first note and hold it through the time value of the next note.

Will the Circle be Unbroken

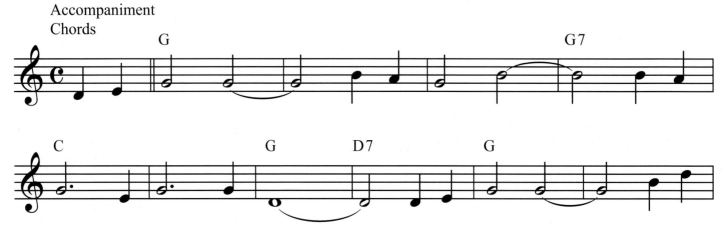

Mama Don't Allow

(No Mandolin Playin' Round Here!)

F#

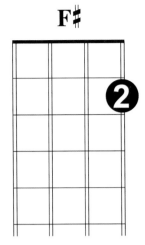

2nd Finger, 1st String, 2nd Fret

2nd Finger, 1st String, 2nd Fret

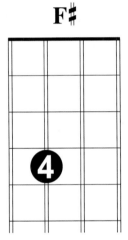

3rd or 4th Finger, 3rd String, 4th Fret

3rd or 4th Finger, 3rd String, 4th Fret

Track 49

Streets of Laredo

Accompaniment
Chords

Bonus Solos
In The Pines

Slowly

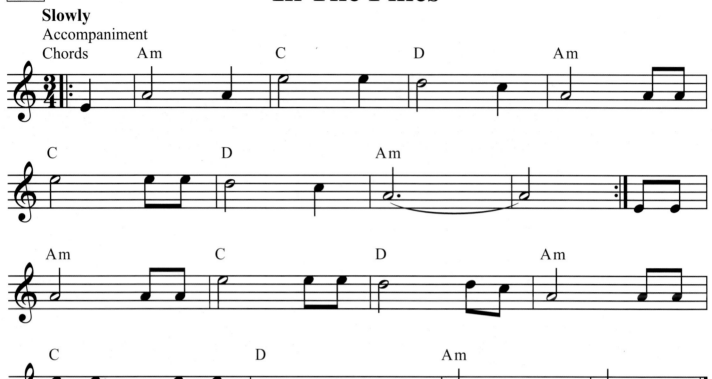

Come and Go with Me
(To that Land where I'm Bound)

Lively tempo

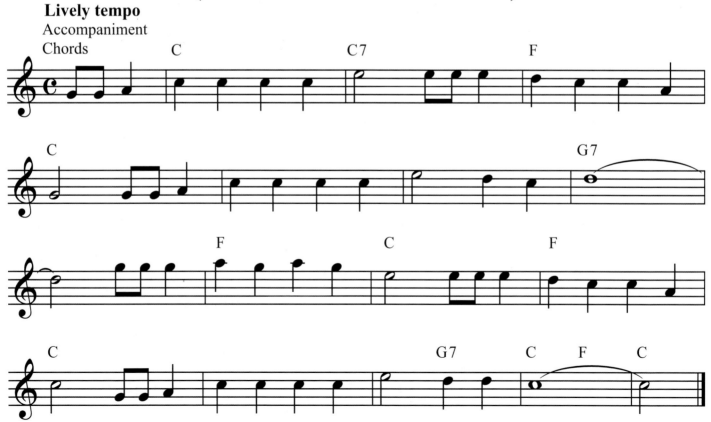

Golden Slippers

Green Grow The Lilacs

Slowly

This Train

Brisk Tempo

It Ain't Gonna Rain No More

Track 56

Jacob's Ladder

Track 57